Twiddlez

Twiddlez

Riddles with a Twist

Hi Jo!

Have fun with Twiddlez

Relax, laugh, learn & smile.

All of my best

God Bless You

Jerry E. Truch

JERRY E. TRUCHAN

ILLUSTRATIONS BY JENNIFER FISHER

To order additional copies of this book, contact:
Xlibris Corporation
1-888-795-4274
www.Xlibris.com
Orders@Xlibris.com
62602

"Twiddlez" is dedicated to my beautiful, gifted, and talented daughter Hilary Kay Truchan who is now attending "Virginia Commonwealth University" in Richmond for her PhD. in Micro-Biology/ Immunology.

"Thank You" Hilary for showing me your love, respect, strength, and courage. All of which have been great learning tools in my own life.
    —"I Love You Hilary and God Bless You!"
    —Dad-e-o

A special "Thank You" to Jenny Fisher who has been my friend for many years and who is responsible for the illustrations in "Twiddlez." "God Bless You Jenny!" You certainly have special talents and gifts that no one else has or ever will!

How to Play Twiddlez

You could say that "Twiddlez" is also a puzzle. The "Mystery" will tell you under what category the "Final Answer" finds its origination. By piecing together the information found under the "Mystery," "Chapter," and "Recovered Clue" sections along with your creativity and imagination, you will somehow arrive at the correct "Final Answer!"

You will find that there are countless ways in which the "Final Answer" may be associated with the information given. Take your time and be willing to talk each "Twiddle" out. "Twiddlez" is designed to be entertaining! It is not an I.Q. test!

Helpful Hints for Playing Twiddlez

1. "Stay Away" from the correct final answers found in the back of the book! You will be disappointed when you find out that you actually knew the answer but you just needed a little more time.
2. A lot of the fun in "Twiddlez" is where you have to take a step back and let the answer come to you!
3. Often you will find that a "twiddle" isn't twisted enough and that there will be no further help or maybe even a joking comment found in the "Recovered Clue" section.
4. All or some part of the "Final Answer" is associated with the given "Chapter."

5. The "Final Answer" may be as simple as switching 1 letter from the information given in the "Chapter."
6. The real object of "Twiddlez" is to relax and have fun!
7. Give yourself credit and unlock and trust in your own creativity and imagination.
8. It's amazing to find out what your creativity and imagination will produce when you let them take over!
9. Any word(s) *italicized* in the "Chapter" section will be "as is" in the "Final Answer."
10. The order of placement of words found in the "Chapter" may not be the same as in the "Final Answer." Some "twiddlez" will be twisted, even after reading the "Recovered Clue."
11. The clues found in the "Recovered Clue" section refers to the "Final Answer" minus any *word(s) italicized* in the "Chapter."
12. You never know what will trigger the correct "Final Answer!"
13. "Not So Fast!" Correct spelling of the "Final Answer" is required!

About the Cover

In my grade school years the cartoon character "Touche Turtle" was very popular. With the last name of "Truchan" I was comically referred to as "Truchan the turtle!" It's been a part of my life that has somehow stayed with me. This is my character on the cover (illustrated by Jenny Fisher) turning on his creativity and imagination.

1. <u>Mystery</u>
Rap/Hip-Hop

   <u>Chapter</u>
   Melts in Your
   Mouth

   <u>Recovered Clue</u>
   Not in your hands

   Final Answer

2. <u>Mystery</u>
Soap Opera

   <u>Chapter</u>
   The Old *and the*
   Not so Hot

   <u>Recovered Clue</u>
   "Oh Brook"
   "Oh Ridge"

   Final Answer

3. <u>Mystery</u>
Major League
Baseball

   <u>Chapter</u>
   See Illustration

   <u>Recovered Clue</u>
   "I have a butter
   stain on my tie!"

   Final Answer

4. <u>Mystery</u>
    Movie Title

    <u>Chapter</u>
    Toot, Toot
    _ _ _ Goodbye

    <u>Recovered Clue</u>
    Chocolaty and
    Chewy

    Final Answer

5. <u>Mystery</u>
    Alcoholic
    Beverage

    <u>Chapter</u>
    Latin Lettuce
    Leaper

    <u>Recovered Clue</u>
    Lawnjumper

    Final Answer

6. <u>Mystery</u>
    Nursery Rhyme

    <u>Chapter</u>
    Mary Has *a* Big
    Goat

    <u>Recovered Clue</u>
    What did she
    do with it?

    Final Answer

7. <u>Mystery</u>
    Foreign Leader

    <u>Chapter</u>
    Violin *Castro*

    <u>Recovered Clue</u>
    A little bit of
    "Foggy Mountain
    Breakdown"
    please!

    Final Answer

8.
<u>Mystery</u>
Female Country/
Western Singer

<u>Chapter</u>
Mark Twain's
Sister?

<u>Recovered Clue</u>
Not Shanaynay!

Final Answer

9.
<u>Mystery</u>
Female/
Mainstream Rock

<u>Chapter</u>
Cheryl Kaw!

<u>Recovered Clues</u>
She rode bikes
with Lance

Final Answer

10.
<u>Mystery</u>
Foreign Country

<u>Chapter</u>
You Roll, I Rock

<u>Recovered Clue</u>
You roll, _ _ _

Final Answer

11.
<u>Mystery</u>
TV Show

<u>Chapter</u>
3,600 Seconds

<u>Recovered Clue</u>
1/168 of a week

Final Answer

12. Mystery
TV Show

Chapter
Home Detonation

Recovered Clue
I never wear
flannel!

Final Answer

13. Mystery
Major League
Baseball

Chapter
Infant Home-Run
Hitter

Recovered Clue
"What are
steroids?"

Final Answer

14. Mystery
Professional
Golfer

Chapter
Green Acres
Pig *Palmer*

Recovered Clue
"I prefer sand
traps to mud."

Final Answer

15. Mystery
Movie Title

Chapter
Precipitation Guy

Recovered Clue
K-Mart,
Judge Wapner

Final Answer

16. **Mystery**
     Movie Title

     Chapter
     Whacko!

     Recovered Clue
     E! E! E!

     Final Answer

17. **Mystery**
     Song Title

     Chapter
     Loose Eel

     Recovered Clue
     U picked a fine time
     to leave me _ _ _

     Final Answer

18. **Mystery**
     Middle East
     History

     Chapter
     Yes Sir, I am Fat

     Recovered Clue
     And not too good
     looking either

     Final Answer

19. **Mystery**
     Italian Fashion
     Designer

     Chapter
     Koochee

     Recovered Clue
     You are on your
     own

     Final Answer

20. Mystery
Actress

Chapter
Do You Think
Natalie Would?

Recovered Clue
Yes! I do

Final Answer

21. Mystery
Motown Artist

Chapter
Marvin Straight

Recovered Clue
In a funny sort of
way

Final Answer

22. Mystery
TV Show

Chapter
Leave it to Badger

Recovered Clue
G Wally

Final Answer

23. Mystery
Movie Title

Chapter
Who Set Up the
Hare?

Recovered Clue
Is that a pic of
Roger on the
wall?

Final Answer

24.   <u>Mystery</u>
Personal Product

      <u>Chapter</u>
Polly's Car Has
a Dent

      <u>Recovered Clue</u>
I am so happy
that I can eat
corn on the cob
now!

      Final Answer

25.   <u>Mystery</u>
Beverage

      <u>Chapter</u>
60 Second Butler

      <u>Recovered Clue</u>
In a minute

      Final Answer

26.   <u>Mystery</u>
Known for Rice

      <u>Chapter</u>
Aunt Franklin

      <u>Recovered Clue</u>
He's so quick!

      Final Answer

27.   <u>Mystery</u>
Comic Strip

      <u>Chapter</u>
Pizza Pimples

      <u>Recovered Clue</u>
I don't even eat
pizza and I still
get them!

      Final Answer

28. <u>Mystery</u>
Italian Cuisine

<u>Chapter</u>
Passda

<u>Recovered Clue</u>
Your clue phone
is ringing!

Final Answer

29. <u>Mystery</u>
Domestic Retailer

<u>Chapter</u>
Air Mattress
Sauna *&* Light
Years Away

<u>Recovered Clue</u>
What more do you
need?

Final Answer

30. <u>Mystery</u>
Bible

<u>Chapter</u>
Occupation

<u>Recovered Clue</u>
It is over rated

Final Answer

31. <u>Mystery</u>
Bible

<u>Chapter</u>
_ _ _ Was a
Bullfrog

<u>Recovered Clue</u>
Was a good friend
of mine.

Final Answer

32. <u>Mystery</u>
Musician

    <u>Chapter</u>
Light-Headed
Gillespie

    <u>Recovered Clue</u>
Who bent
his horn?

    Final Answer

33. <u>Mystery</u>
Alcoholic
Beverage

    <u>Chapter</u>
Triumphant
Boxer
Throws It

    <u>Recovered Clue</u>
Not below the
belt please!

    Final Answer

34. <u>Mystery</u>
Song Title

    <u>Chapter</u>
Like a Sturgeon

    <u>Recovered Clue</u>
The "v" word

    Final Answer

35. <u>Mystery</u>
Song Title

    <u>Chapter</u>
If You Had ESP

    <u>Recovered Clue</u>
I'd be in big
trouble!

    Final Answer

36. <u>Mystery</u>
TV Canine

<u>Chapter</u>
Tin Rin Rin

<u>Recovered Clue</u>
Change (3) letters

Final Answer

37. <u>Mystery</u>
Famous Street

<u>Chapter</u>
Bronco Busting
Drive

<u>Recovered Clue</u>
Oh Mumzee!

Final Answer

38. <u>Mystery</u>
National Football
League

<u>Chapter</u>
See Illustration

<u>Recovered Clue</u>
I need at least
1 cup in the
morning!

Final Answer

39. Mystery
    Poet

    Chapter
    Shortguy

    Recovered Clue
    Do you mean
    tall?

    Final Answer

40. Mystery
    Mythology

    Chapter
    Comet

    Recovered Clue
    Ajills

    Final Answer

41. Mystery
    Actor

    Chapter
    Erik Chiquita

    Recovered Clue
    Robert Dole
    knows him

    Final Answer

42. Mystery
    Actor

    Chapter
    Go Ahead and
    Make My Day

    Recovered Clue
    Lights, camera,
    action

    Final Answer

43. <u>Mystery</u>
TV Show Host

<u>Chapter</u>
Dr. Full

<u>Recovered Clue</u>
Fill it up!

Final Answer

44. <u>Mystery</u>
Actress

<u>Chapter</u>
Judy Glitter

<u>Recovered Clue</u>
"There's no place like home!"

Final Answer

45. <u>Mystery</u>
Actress

<u>Chapter</u>
Sketched Less
Strawberries

<u>Recovered Clue</u>
Take your time on this one!

Final Answer

46. <u>Mystery</u>
Credit Card

<u>Chapter</u>
Christopher
Columbus

<u>Recovered Clue</u>
Look what I found!

Final Answer

47.   Mystery
        International
        Food

        Chapter
        32,000 oz. *Soup*

        Recovered Clue
        How many ton's
        is that?

        Final Answer

48.   Mystery
        Newspaper

        Chapter
        The Vidalia

        Recovered Clue
        It will make you
        cry!

        Final Answer

49.   Mystery
        Illness

        Chapter
        The Bacon Flew

        Recovered Clue
        In a pig's ear!

        Final Answer

50.   Mystery
        Food Seasoning

        Chapter
        Parsley, Sage,
        Rosemary and _ _ _

        Recovered Clue
        What time is it?

        Final Answer

51.   Mystery
       Condiment

       Chapter
       Throwup

       Recovered Clue
       You go ahead, I'll
       catch up!

       Final Answer

52.   Mystery
       Barbecue Utensil

       Chapter
       _ _ _! Didn't Even
       Know Her!

       Recovered Clue
       Does Bob know
       how to shishka?

       Final Answer

53.   Mystery
       International
       Food

       Chapter
       Cold Today,
       Hot _ _ _

       Recovered Clue
       Are weather
       forecasters ever
       right?

       Final Answer

54.   Mystery
       Dominica Food

       Chapter
       I Can't Breathe,
       Cluck, Cluck!

       Recovered Clue
       Here I come
       Colonel!

       Final Answer

55. **Mystery**
U.S. University

Chapter
In Wisconsin?

Recovered Clue
University of
Cudahy on the
Lake Almost

Final Answer

56. **Mystery**
Famous Square

Chapter
Jolly Good
Ol' Chap

Recovered Clue
Don't dilly dally
around

Final Answer

57. **Mystery**
European History

Chapter
Steak Sauce
Hitler

Recovered Clue
Talk about
someone who
needs a new
hairstylist!

Final Answer

58. **Mystery**
Scientist

Chapter
Lewis Grazing
Land

Recovered Clue
Does he
pasteurize?

Final Answer

59. <u>Mystery</u>
Major League
Baseball

<u>Chapter</u>
Musty
Candlestick
Maker

<u>Recovered Clue</u>
"May I use your
toothpick?"

Final Answer

60. <u>Mystery</u>
Famous Artist

<u>Chapter</u>
Vincent Cargo _ _ _
Green Light

<u>Recovered Clue</u>
Stop!

Final Answer

61. <u>Mystery</u>
Electronics

<u>Chapter</u>
I'm Entitled to 1
Phone Call!

<u>Recovered Clue</u>
Use your _ _ _
in your _ _ _!

Final Answer

62. <u>Mystery</u>
Female Recording
Artist

<u>Chapter</u>
Are You Positive?

<u>Recovered Clue</u>
No doubt!

Final Answer

63. Mystery
     Province

     Chapter
     I Found a New
     Land

     Recovered Clue
     Ding! Ding! Ding!

     Final Answer

64. Mystery
     West African City

     Chapter
     Tim has $2.00

     Recovered Clue
     Named after him?

     Final Answer

65. Mystery
     TV Show

     Chapter
     Scours

     Recovered Clue
     Appletinis

     Final Answer

66. Mystery
     TV Show

     Chapter
     Half as Good
     as 5 Women?

     Recovered Clue
     Figure it out

     Final Answer

67.   <u>Mystery</u>   68.   <u>Mystery</u>
       Major League   Excellent Dining
       Baseball   in Cedarburg, WI

       <u>Chapter</u>   <u>Chapter</u>
       Braden, Y Such   Let's Go to
       a Long Face?   *The* _ _ _ Instead

       <u>Recovered Clue</u>   <u>Recovered Clue</u>
       Excellent pitcher   Angie & Kelly

       Final Answer   *Final Answer*

69.   <u>Mystery</u>
       Movie Title

       <u>Chapter</u>
       See Illustration

       <u>Recovered Clue</u>
       What's the curfew
       for cowboys?

       Final Answer

70. Mystery
TV Character

Chapter
_ _ _, You've Got
Some Splainin' To
Do!

Recovered Clue
"Buzz off Ricky!"

Final Answer

71. Mystery
TV Game Show

Chapter
Inner Tube
of Cookie

Recovered Clue
Whoa! Vanna!

Final Answer

72. Mystery
Illness

Chapter
Out Flew N Za

Recovered Clue
Usually goes
both ways!

Final Answer

73. Mystery
Narcotic

Chapter
Mr. Nick O. Teen

Recovered Clue
I know it's
killing me but I
absolutely
love it!

Final Answer

74. <u>Mystery</u>
Human Organ

<u>Chapter</u>
What's the Matter
With Your _ _ _?

<u>Recovered Clue</u>
It Depends!

Final Answer

75. <u>Mystery</u>
Human Tissue

<u>Chapter</u>
Frosty the
Snowman
Bit Me!

<u>Recovered Clue</u>
Now I've got _ _ _!

Final Answer

76. <u>Mystery</u>
Illness

<u>Chapter</u>
Ted Nugent Song

<u>Recovered Clue</u>
Take a pill!

Final Answer

77. <u>Mystery</u>
Human Virus

<u>Chapter</u>
Asphalt _ _ _

<u>Recovered Clue</u>
30 year warranty

Final Answer

78. <u>Mystery</u>
Female Rock
Figurehead

<u>Chapter</u>
Joan Air Force 1

<u>Recovered Clue</u>
Black box

Final Answer

79. <u>Mystery</u>
Actor/Comedian

<u>Chapter</u>
Billy Watch
Dial Cover

<u>Recovered Clue</u>
Sapphire or
plastic

Final Answer

80. <u>Mystery</u>
Actor

<u>Chapter</u>
Christopher
Electrician

<u>Recovered Clue</u>
3 ¼ inch flush
valve

Final Answer

81. <u>Mystery</u>
American Idol

<u>Chapter</u>
I Love the
Sauerkraut!

<u>Recovered Clue</u>
Corned-beef
sandwich

Final Answer

82. <u>Mystery</u>
Male R&B/Rap/
Pop

<u>Chapter</u>
Usha

<u>Recovered Clue</u>
Pass the basket
all of the way
down please!

Final Answer

83. <u>Mystery</u>
Human Illness

<u>Chapter</u>
Septic *Ulcer*

<u>Recovered Clue</u>
Don't take
"Rid-ex!"

Final Answer

84. <u>Mystery</u>
Comic Strip

<u>Chapter</u>
Zaggy

<u>Recovered Clue</u>
I zagged when
I should have
zigged!

Final Answer

85. <u>Mystery</u>
Rock n' Roll
Group

<u>Chapter</u>
Spy Plane

<u>Recovered Clue</u>
Me also?

Final Answer

86. <u>Mystery</u>
Foreign Country

<u>Chapter</u>
I Did it Myuguay!

<u>Recovered Clue</u>
Youruguay?

Final Answer

87. <u>Mystery</u>
French Polynesian
Island

<u>Chapter</u>
Yawna Yawna

<u>Recovered Clue</u>
Actually, it was
quite exciting!

Final Answer

88. <u>Mystery</u>
U.S. City

<u>Chapter</u>
Picante Sauce

<u>Recovered Clue</u>
Is this city
on No-Doz?

Final Answer

89. <u>Mystery</u>
Principality

<u>Chapter</u>
Orca

<u>Recovered Clue</u>
Whales

Final Answer

90. <u>Mystery</u>
Kidz-TV

<u>Chapter</u>
Who Stole My
Sweater?

<u>Recovered Clue</u>
Mrs. Rogers Hood

Final Answer

91. <u>Mystery</u>
Kidz TV

<u>Chapter</u>
Bzzzzt!

<u>Recovered Clue</u>
Get out of that
water!

Final Answer

92. <u>Mystery</u>
National
Basketball
Association

<u>Chapter</u>
Mark Castro

<u>Recovered Clue</u>
There are
similarities!

Final Answer

93. <u>Mystery</u>
Internet Site

<u>Chapter</u>
Mug-Shot Book

<u>Recovered Clue</u>
Not for when you
get arrested!

Final Answer

94. <u>Mystery</u>
Pro-Wrestling

<u>Chapter</u>
Verne Gagme

<u>Recovered Clue</u>
"The Sleeper,"
it should be
outlawed!

Final Answer

95. <u>Mystery</u>
Major-League
Baseball

<u>Chapter</u>
The South-Side
Knee-Highs

<u>Recovered Clue</u>
I can't understand
the manager!

Final Answer

96. <u>Mystery</u>
National Football
League

<u>Chapter</u>
Breakfast Drink
Homer

<u>Recovered Clue</u>
"It doesn't fit!"

Final Answer

97. <u>Mystery</u>
Pro-Golfers
Association

<u>Chapter</u>
Chip Baldo

<u>Recovered Clue</u>
The faldo thru is
very important!

Final Answer

98. <u>Mystery</u>
National Hockey
League

<u>Chapter</u>
Gal La Flower

<u>Recovered Clue</u>
I told u that it
pays to know
about hockey!

Final Answer

99. <u>Mystery</u>
Olympian

<u>Chapter</u>
Bruce Kardashian

<u>Recovered Clue</u>
Mr. Facelift

Final Answer

100. <u>Mystery</u>
National
Basketball
Association

<u>Chapter</u>
Earl the Pearl _ _ _

<u>Recovered Clue</u>
He does struts
too!

Final Answer

101. <u>Mystery</u>
Olympian

<u>Chapter</u>
Edwin "Ten
Commandments"

<u>Recovered Clue</u>
Where's my stick?

Final Answer

102. <u>Mystery</u>
Female Czech
Entrepreneur

<u>Chapter</u>
I Vant to Play
Sheepshead!

<u>Recovered Clue</u>
"I couldn't stand
his hairpiece!"

Final Answer

103. <u>Mystery</u>
National Football
League

<u>Chapter</u>
Dick Keesterkisser

<u>Recovered Clue</u>
That's 1 way
of saying it!

Final Answer

104. <u>Mystery</u>
Movie Title

<u>Chapter</u>
See Illustration

<u>Recovered Clue</u>
Now I've
seen it all!

Final Answer

105. Mystery
Movie Title

Chapter
Oh My Ga *Girl*

Recovered Clue
San Fernando _ _ _

Final Answer

106. Mystery
Musical

Chapter
Illegally Brunette

Recovered Clue
But it's natural!

Final Answer

107. Mystery
Cable Television

Chapter
13th, 20th, & 22'nd
Letters of the
Alphabet

Recovered Clue
Sorry! ☺

Final Answer

108. Mystery
TV Show

Chapter
Where Should We
Put That Kid?

Recovered Clue
Do you mean
Malcolm?

Final Answer

109. Mystery
Song Title

Chapter
I Want My CNN

Recovered Clue
The clue phone
is ringing ☺

Final Answer

110. Mystery
Song Title

Chapter
Run *Like*
a Kenyan

Recovered Clue
Walk, don't run

Final Answer

111. Mystery
Working Dog

Chapter
Your *Collie*
Needs a Shave

Recovered Clue
It's a girl!

Final Answer

112. Mystery
Male Vocal

Chapter
Don Garden Tool

Recovered Clue
I saw him working
the street!

Final Answer

113. <u>Mystery</u>
Traffic Sign

<u>Chapter</u>
Cross Dresser
Does Not Stop

<u>Recovered Clue</u>
Look both ways

Final Answer

114. <u>Mystery</u>
Traffic Sign

<u>Chapter</u>
Oh Wow Man
Limit 65

<u>Recovered Clue</u>
What do they
call it now?

Final Answer

115. <u>Mystery</u>
Professional Golf
Association

<u>Chapter</u>
See Illustration

<u>Recovered Clue</u>
Do you think
he woulds?

Final Answer

116. <u>Mystery</u>
Musical
Instrument

<u>Chapter</u>
2 Sheep

<u>Recovered Clue</u>
Baaaaaaaaaah!

Final Answer

117. <u>Mystery</u>
Musical
Instrument

<u>Chapter</u>
Large and Small
Mouth _ _ _oon

<u>Recovered Clue</u>
I fish for
bottle bass

Final Answer

118. <u>Mystery</u>
Fowl

<u>Chapter</u>
Shut Up! It's
Only Dawn!

<u>Recovered Clue</u>
Foghorn Leghorn

Final Answer

119. <u>Mystery</u>
Mongolian Canine

<u>Chapter</u>
_ _ _ Mein
_ _ _ Mein

<u>Recovered Clue</u>
Purina Dog _ _ _

Final Answer

120. <u>Mystery</u>
Song Title

<u>Chapter</u>
I Only Have
Pupils *For You*

<u>Recovered Clue</u>
The I's have it!

Final Answer

121. <u>Mystery</u>
Alcoholic
Beverage

<u>Chapter</u>
Shaken, Not
Stirred

<u>Recovered Clue</u>
It cleans out
pipes too!

Final Answer

122. <u>Mystery</u>
Alcoholic
Beverage

<u>Chapter</u>
Make Sure You
Rinse Off!

<u>Recovered Clue</u>
Getting frisky on
the beach

Final Answer

123. <u>Mystery</u>
Women in History

<u>Chapter</u>
Betty Floss

<u>Recovered Clue</u>
I think she did
between each star
and stripe

Final Answer

124. <u>Mystery</u>
Artist

<u>Chapter</u>
White Teeth

<u>Recovered Clue</u>
You'll need
a brush also!

Final Answer

125. <u>Mystery</u>
AWA Wrestler

<u>Chapter</u>
Ric Rollerball

<u>Recovered Clue</u>
I thought he had
that certain way
about him!

Final Answer

126. <u>Mystery</u>
AWA Wrestler

<u>Chapter</u>
Dick the
Schmoozer

<u>Recovered Clue</u>
"Where's da
Crusher?"

Final Answer

127. <u>Mystery</u>
WWF Wrestler

<u>Chapter</u>
Alexis Booger

<u>Recovered Clue</u>
German WW2
pistol

Final Answer

128. <u>Mystery</u>
Human Disease

<u>Chapter</u>
O. B. City

<u>Recovered Clue</u>
Nobody makes
me eat

Final Answer

129. <u>Mystery</u>
Paper Product

<u>Chapter</u>
This is Good
for Dirty Necks

<u>Recovered Clue</u>
Oh! I get it!

Final Answer

130. <u>Mystery</u>
Cooking
Ingredient

<u>Chapter</u>
I Can't Find
the *Milk*!

<u>Recovered Clue</u>
That's why they
call it

Final Answer

131. <u>Mystery</u>
Fruit

<u>Chapter</u>
You Have to Get
Married Here,
You _ _ _.

<u>Recovered Clue</u>
But it's less
expensive!

Final Answer

132. Mystery
Cable TV

Chapter
The Oh Really
Factor

Recovered Clue
Well bless my
lucky charms

Final Answer

133. Mystery
National Hockey
League

Chapter
Mario Lebark

Recovered Clue
Alright! A cat
fight!

Final Answer

134. Mystery
Cable TV

Chapter
The Cradle
Robber

Recovered Clue
Not with my son
you hussie!

Final Answer

135. Mystery
Soap Opera

Chapter
They're Not
Your Kids!

Recovered Clue
Thank goodness

Final Answer

136. <u>Mystery</u>
Cable TV

<u>Chapter</u>
Extra Sensory
Perception
Network

<u>Recovered Clue</u>
How did you
know?

Final Answer

137. <u>Mystery</u>
Bitter Alkaloid

<u>Chapter</u>
Calfeen

<u>Recovered Clue</u>
I just have
to have it!

Final Answer

138. <u>Mystery</u>
Soap Opera

<u>Chapter</u>
One Life to Flush

<u>Recovered Clue</u>
Same thing
on that show

Final Answer

139. <u>Mystery</u>
Actor/Comedian

<u>Chapter</u>
David Club

<u>Recovered Clue</u>
Do you play
cards?

Final Answer

140. Mystery
Great Roman
Emperor

Chapter
Is *Marcus*
for Realius?

Recovered Clue
For real!

Final Answer

141. Mystery
Roman History

Chapter
Foe of Popeye
& Julius Caesar

Recovered Clue
He wears BRUT

Final Answer

142. Mystery
Mythology

Chapter
Midnight at the _ _ _

Recovered Clue
A Paulo?

Final Answer

143. Mystery
Health

Chapter
What? I Need
a What?

Recovered Clue
I can't hear you!

Final Answer

144. Mystery
Neurotransmitter

Chapter
You're No Dope
of Mine!

Recovered Clue
Why, thank you!

Final Answer

145. Mystery
Oral Health

Chapter
I'll Have a Gin and
Givitis on the Rocks

Recovered Clue
Tastes like a
Christmas tree.

Final Answer

146. Mystery
Skin Condition

Chapter
Acme

Recovered Clue
Watch your diet!

Final Answer

147. Mystery
Illness

Chapter
Oldmonia

Recovered Clue
But I just bought
it new!

Final Answer

148. Mystery
Human Muscle

Chapter
3 Ceps

Recovered Clue
Tri again!

Final Answer

149. Mystery
Traffic Sign

Chapter
Eggzit *Only*

Recovered Clue
Do Not Enter

Final Answer

150. Mystery
Flower

Chapter
More Than 1
Kramer
From Seinfeld

Recovered Clue
I like mine with
an olive.

Final Answer

151. Mystery
Male Hip-Hop

Chapter
Fity Sen

Recovered Clue
Say what?

Final Answer

152. <u>Mystery</u>
1'st Country/
Western
American Idol

<u>Chapter</u>
Cash and _ _ _
Underwood

<u>Recovered Clue</u>
Carry out
available

Final Answer

153. <u>Mystery</u>
Human Anatomy

<u>Chapter</u>
You're a Nary
Tract!

<u>Recovered Clue</u>
I drink a lot of
cranberry juice!

Final Answer

154. <u>Mystery</u>
Hip-Hop

<u>Chapter</u>
See Illustration

<u>Recovered Clue</u>
But jars can't
hear!

Final Answer

155. <u>Mystery</u>
Birds of a Feather

<u>Chapter</u>
That *Owl* Has
Long Ears

<u>Recovered Clue</u>
Would a
hyphen help?

Final Answer

156. <u>Mystery</u>
Birds of a Feather

<u>Chapter</u>
Chuck Connors
as the _ _ _

<u>Recovered Clue</u>
Paw, do you always
wear a long-sleeved
shirt?

Final Answer

157. <u>Mystery</u>
Birds of a Feather

<u>Chapter</u>
Blew 10th Letter of
the Alphabet

<u>Recovered Clue</u>
Plays baseball
in Toronto

Final Answer

158. <u>Mystery</u>
Birds of a Feather

<u>Chapter</u>
Who *Painted*
That *Bunting*?

<u>Recovered Clue</u>
Does it matter?

Final Answer

159. <u>Mystery</u>
Chess

<u>Chapter</u>
Type of Crow
and Chess Piece

<u>Recovered Clue</u>
Can only fly side
to side and front
to back

Final Answer

160. <u>Mystery</u>
Human Race

<u>Chapter</u>
Asian Crow

<u>Recovered Clue</u>
Or crow asian

Final Answer

161. <u>Mystery</u>
Medical
Dictionary

<u>Chapter</u>
She Played the
Banjo
on Her Knee

<u>Recovered Clue</u>
a

Final Answer

162. <u>Mystery</u>
Disease

<u>Chapter</u>
Mr. Al K. Haulic

<u>Recovered Clue</u>
Was it named
after him?

Final Answer

163. Mystery
      Medicine

      Chapter
      Are You Against
      Biotics?

      Recovered Clue
      No, I take them
      all of the time.

      Final Answer

164. Mystery
      Illness

      Chapter
      John Denver
      Spotted Fever

      Recovered Clue
      _ _ _ high,
      Colorado

      Final Answer

165. Mystery
      Human Anatomy

      Chapter
      Didn't Even
      Know Her

      Recovered Clue
      Darn near
      wrecked 'em

      Final Answer

166. Mystery
      Foot Condition

      Chapter
      Your *Feet* Must
      Have a Leak

      Recovered Clue
      Do you have a
      spare?

      Final Answer

167. <u>Mystery</u>
Sports Ailment

<u>Chapter</u>
Every *Tennis*
Player Has One

<u>Recovered Clue</u>
Actually 2

Final Answer

168. <u>Mystery</u>
Female Model

<u>Chapter</u>
Kate Floss

<u>Recovered Clue</u>
Only on the
north side!

Final Answer

169. <u>Mystery</u>
Actress

<u>Chapter</u>
Sandra Oh

<u>Recovered Clue</u>
O my

Final Answer

170. <u>Mystery</u>
Country Western
Singer

<u>Chapter</u>
Tirty Pointer

<u>Recovered Clue</u>
Doe Owens

Final Answer

171. <u>Mystery</u>
satan Superstar

<u>Chapter</u>
Related to
Charles *Manson*?

<u>Recovered Clue</u>
It runs in
the family

Final Answer

172. <u>Mystery</u>
Country Western
Singer

<u>Chapter</u>
Tammy No Way

<u>Recovered Clue</u>
Y not?

Final Answer

173. <u>Mystery</u>
U.K. Grammy
Winner

<u>Chapter</u>
A. Me Vineyard

<u>Recovered Clue</u>
"I said no, no, no!"

Final Answer

174. <u>Mystery</u>
U.S. City

<u>Chapter</u>
_ _ _ Omelette

<u>Recovered Clue</u>
John _ _ _

Final Answer

175. <u>Mystery</u>
Foreign City

<u>Chapter</u>
_ _ _ Sprouts

<u>Recovered Clue</u>
Yuk!

Final Answer

176. <u>Mystery</u>
Foreign City

<u>Chapter</u>
Pilot to
Bombardier

<u>Recovered Clue</u>
Open the
_ _ _ doors

Final Answer

177. <u>Mystery</u>
Foreign Country

<u>Chapter</u>
Kooba

<u>Recovered Clue</u>
Gooding

Final Answer

178. <u>Mystery</u>
Spanish Islands

<u>Chapter</u>
Tweety Bird

<u>Recovered Clue</u>
Putuliar

Final Answer

179. <u>Mystery</u>
U.S. City

<u>Chapter</u>
Bruce
Springsteen
32,000 Ounces

<u>Recovered Clue</u>
Say "No" to
calculators

Final Answer

180. <u>Mystery</u>
U.S. State

<u>Chapter</u>
I'm Fine

<u>Recovered Clue</u>
How are you?

Final Answer

181. <u>Mystery</u>
European City

<u>Chapter</u>
Oh Da Terlet

<u>Recovered Clue</u>
Perfume

Final Answer

182. <u>Mystery</u>
Foreign Country

<u>Chapter</u>
Gyros

<u>Recovered Clue</u>
Grease

Final Answer

183. <u>Mystery</u>
Famous
Boulevard

<u>Chapter</u>
What is Santa's
Last Name?

<u>Recovered Clue</u>
Sheryl Crow
sings about it

Final Answer

184. <u>Mystery</u>
Foreign City

<u>Chapter</u>
Big Ben

<u>Recovered Clue</u>
☺

Final Answer

185. <u>Mystery</u>
U.S. City

<u>Chapter</u>
_ _ _ Slugger

<u>Recovered Clue</u>
Kentucky
Cardinals

Final Answer

186. <u>Mystery</u>
Foreign Country

<u>Chapter</u>
Uwalked

<u>Recovered Clue</u>
Keep running

Final Answer

187. <u>Mystery</u>
Foreign City

<u>Chapter</u>
Day Old Bakery

<u>Recovered Clue</u>
Fresh creamy
coleslaw

Final Answer

188. <u>Mystery</u>
U.S. City

<u>Chapter</u>
And Your Little
Dog Too!

<u>Recovered Clue</u>
The wicked _ _ _
of the west

Final Answer

189. <u>Mystery</u>
U.S. City

<u>Chapter</u>
Mickeyapolis

<u>Recovered Clue</u>
Minniesota

Final Answer

190. <u>Mystery</u>
Traffic Sign

<u>Chapter</u>
I'm so Tired, I'm
Gonna _ _ _
Investigation Site

<u>Recovered Clue</u>
Clyde _ _ _cup

Final Answer

191. <u>Mystery</u>
Actor

<u>Chapter</u>
Judy, Judy, Judy

<u>Recovered Clue</u>
Please grant Cary
his wish.

Final Answer

192. <u>Mystery</u>
Actor

<u>Chapter</u>
Kevin Macon

<u>Recovered Clue</u>
When pigs fly!

Final Answer

193. <u>Mystery</u>
Actor/Comedian

<u>Chapter</u>
John _ _ _ and
Dentists Best
Friend

<u>Recovered Clue</u>
Sweet!

Final Answer

194. <u>Mystery</u>
University

<u>Chapter</u>
William _ _ _ *State*

<u>Recovered Clue</u>
Fountain _ _ _

Final Answer

195. <u>Mystery</u>
Flower

<u>Chapter</u>
I Can't Wait!

<u>Recovered Clue</u>
Patience is a
virtue

Final Answer

196. <u>Mystery</u>
Magazine

<u>Chapter</u>
Tell Me About Your
Childhood *Today*

<u>Recovered Clue</u>
Lay on the
couch please

Final Answer

197. <u>Mystery</u>
Duck

<u>Chapter</u>
Pin the Tail on
the Donkey

<u>Recovered Clue</u>
It works on
ducks too!

Final Answer

198. <u>Mystery</u>
Birds of the Air

<u>Chapter</u>
Harry *Woodpecker*

<u>Recovered Clue</u>
What r u
waiting 4?

Final Answer

199. <u>Mystery</u>
Birds of the Air

<u>Chapter</u>
Missiletoebird

<u>Recovered Clue</u>
Christmas
smooch

Final Answer

200. <u>Mystery</u>
Traffic Sign

<u>Chapter</u>
No Public
Restroom

<u>Recovered Clue</u>
Does this include
animals?

Final Answer

201. <u>Mystery</u>
Soap Opera

<u>Chapter</u>
General Day
Care Center

<u>Recovered Clue</u>
They all need
help!

Final Answer

202. <u>Mystery</u>
Predatory Bird

<u>Chapter</u>
Yul Brenner *Eagle*

<u>Recovered Clue</u>
Balled

Final Answer

203. Mystery
     Actor

     Chapter
     Third Degree _ _ _

     Recovered Clue
     Georgie Porgie

     Final Answer

204. Mystery
     Actor

     Chapter
     Salad Dressing
     Guy

     Recovered Clue
     Saul

     Final Answer

205. Mystery
     Actor

     Chapter
     Andy Taylor

     Recovered Clue
     Omar

     Final Answer

206. Mystery
     Actor

     Chapter
     George _ _ _knee

     Recovered Clue
     Get a _ _ _

     Final Answer

207. <u>Mystery</u>
Late Nite TV Host

<u>Chapter</u>
David Goes Postal

<u>Recovered Clue</u>
"Top 10 reasons
why you should
deliver mail!"

Final Answer

208. <u>Mystery</u>
TV Show

<u>Chapter</u>
How I Dumped
Your Father

<u>Recovered Clue</u>
I didn't drink
that much!

Final Answer

209. <u>Mystery</u>
TV Character

<u>Chapter</u>
See Illustration

<u>Recovered Clue</u>
Warp Speed
Scottie!

Final Answer

210. Mystery
Actress/Singer

Chapter
Las Vegas *Midler*

Recovered Clue
Wanna bet!

Final Answer

211. Mystery
Cable TV

Chapter
The E! Total Waste
of Time *Story*

Recovered Clue
That's a better
name!

Final Answer

212. Mystery
Actress

Chapter
_ _ _ Hen

Recovered Clue
Dear Abbey

Final Answer

213. Mystery
Reality TV Figure

Chapter
Kate Gooselin

Recovered Clue
Same # of letters

Final Answer

214. Mystery
     Actress

     Chapter
     Farrah Faucet

     Recovered Clue
     Homonym

     Final Answer

215. Mystery
     Actress

     Chapter
     It's a *Temple* and
     Don't Call Me
     Shirley

     Recovered Clue
     "I would like
     a lollipop!"

     Final Answer

216. Mystery
     Actress

     Chapter
     Layton Youster

     Recovered Clue
     It's all about mc!

     Final Answer

217. Mystery
     Great Musical
     Duo

     Chapter
     I Rented a U-_ _ _
     for Moving

     Recovered Clue
     Quaker makes his
     meal out of this

     Final Answer

218. <u>Mystery</u>
Rock n' Roll Great

<u>Chapter</u>
Ground Round
Barry

<u>Recovered Clue</u>
Less expensive

Final Answer

219. <u>Mystery</u>
American Male
Icon

<u>Chapter</u>
Stevie Judkins

<u>Recovered Clue</u>
I wonder who
this could be?

Final Answer

220. <u>Mystery</u>
English Lead
Singer

<u>Chapter</u>
Mack Jigger

<u>Recovered Clue</u>
Switch 2 letters

Final Answer

221. <u>Mystery</u>
Male Hip-Hop

<u>Chapter</u>
Ridiculous

<u>Recovered Clue</u>
Step into the
21'st century

Final Answer

222. <u>Mystery</u>
Male Hip-Hop

<u>Chapter</u>
Soldier *Boy*

<u>Recovered Clue</u>
Say it from
your soul!

Final Answer

223. <u>Mystery</u>
Hardcore Rap
King

<u>Chapter</u>
4th, 13th, & 24th
Letters of the
Alphabet

<u>Recovered Clue</u>
Use your fingers

Final Answer

224. <u>Mystery</u>
Teen Star

<u>Chapter</u>
Zachary F. Ron

<u>Recovered Clue</u>
Zac

Final Answer

225. <u>Mystery</u>
Country/Western
Vocal

<u>Chapter</u>
Wayne *Brooks*

<u>Recovered Clue</u>
Party on Wayne,
Party on _ _ _

Final Answer

226. <u>Mystery</u>
Male Rock
Performer

<u>Chapter</u>
Chocolate Seal
Point *Stevens*

<u>Recovered Clue</u>
Dane County WI
Friends of Ferals

Final Answer

227. <u>Mystery</u>
Male Rock
Composer

<u>Chapter</u>
Mothers of
Invention

<u>Recovered Clue</u>
Frank Zippo

Final Answer

228. <u>Mystery</u>
Hip-Hop Artist

<u>Chapter</u>
Sunshine State

<u>Recovered Clue</u>
Where's the
hyphen?

Final Answer

229. <u>Mystery</u>
Cable TV

<u>Chapter</u>
Disney Channel
Star

<u>Recovered Clue</u>
Smiley Cyrus

Final Answer

230. <u>Mystery</u>
Hip-Hop Artist

<u>Chapter</u>
_ _ *Cool* _

<u>Recovered Clue</u>
Add 3 letters of
the alphabet

Final Answer

231. <u>Mystery</u>
Male Vocal

<u>Chapter</u>
_ _ _, Over & Out

<u>Recovered Clue</u>
It's Mueller time!

Final Answer

232. <u>Mystery</u>
TV Game Show

<u>Chapter</u>
The Hatfields and
the McCoys

<u>Recovered Clue</u>
Don't you think
it's time that our
families made
up?

Final Answer

233. <u>Mystery</u>
Female Hip-Hop

<u>Chapter</u>
Lady Goo-Goo

<u>Recovered Clue</u>
Complete your
thought

Final Answer

234. Mystery
     Female Gospel

     Chapter
     Merry Merry

     Recovered Clue
     Quite contrary

     Final Answer

235. Mystery
     Female Hip-Hop

     Chapter
     Tastes Very Good

     Recovered Clue
     Delicious

     Final Answer

236. Mystery
     Female Vocal

     Chapter
     Are You Ready?

     Recovered Clue
     Who, Helen?

     Final Answer

237. Mystery
     U.S. City

     Chapter
     Geronimoapolis

     Recovered Clue
     Indiana wants me

     Final Answer

238. <u>Mystery</u>
Foreign Country

<u>Chapter</u>
Stuff It!

<u>Recovered Clue</u>
Gobble, gobble

Final Answer

239. <u>Mystery</u>
Mystery TV Show

<u>Chapter</u>
The Whackoist

<u>Recovered Clue</u>
Use your head!

Final Answer

240. <u>Mystery</u>
U.S. City

<u>Chapter</u>
It's in 10 I C

<u>Recovered Clue</u>
_ _ _ choo choo

Final Answer

241. <u>Mystery</u>
Foreign City

<u>Chapter</u>
Do U Wanna?

<u>Recovered Clue</u>
C senor

Final Answer

242. <u>Mystery</u>
U.S. City

<u>Chapter</u>
By the Time I
Get to _ _ _

<u>Recovered Clue</u>
Home of the Suns

Final Answer

243. <u>Mystery</u>
U.S. City

<u>Chapter</u>
Square Root
of 4son

<u>Recovered Clue</u>
☺

Final Answer

244. <u>Mystery</u>
Foreign City

<u>Chapter</u>
satan's Wash
Basin

<u>Recovered Clue</u>
In Finland?

Final Answer

245. <u>Mystery</u>
Philippine City

<u>Chapter</u>
Thrilla in _ _ _

<u>Recovered Clue</u>
Not vanilla!

Final Answer

246. <u>Mystery</u>
U.S. City

<u>Chapter</u>
This is Where I do
My Shooshing!

<u>Recovered Clue</u>
Bootiepencil

Final Answer

247. <u>Mystery</u>
Kidz TV

<u>Chapter</u>
Carpetmice

<u>Recovered Clue</u>
Use your Rug
Doctor

Final Answer

248. <u>Mystery</u>
Cable TV

<u>Chapter</u>
Ka Blewee!

<u>Recovered Clue</u>
3 powerful letters

Final Answer

249. <u>Mystery</u>
Christian TV

<u>Chapter</u>
The Square Root of
490,000 *Club*

<u>Recovered Clue</u>
That's a great
3 game series!

Final Answer

250. <u>Mystery</u>
Fish

<u>Chapter</u>
Malted Barley
Husband

<u>Recovered Clue</u>
They stink to
high, high
heaven!

Final Answer

251. <u>Mystery</u>
Song Title

<u>Chapter</u>
Good 2 *the*
Marrow

<u>Recovered Clue</u>
J.C.M.

Final Answer

252. <u>Mystery</u>
Hip-Hop Tune

<u>Chapter</u>
Stupid

<u>Recovered Clue</u>
Don't you know
how to spell?

Final Answer

253. <u>Mystery</u>
Hip-Hop Tune

<u>Chapter</u>
Old Maid *Face*

<u>Recovered Clue</u>
Texas Hold'em

Final Answer

254. <u>Mystery</u>
Alcoholic
Beverage

<u>Chapter</u>
White Cosmonaut

<u>Recovered Clue</u>
Nyet!

Final Answer

255. <u>Mystery</u>
Beverage

<u>Chapter</u>
Gilligan's Favorite

<u>Recovered Clue</u>
Plentiful in Samoa

Final Answer

256. <u>Mystery</u>
Alcoholic
Beverage

<u>Chapter</u>
Are You Under
the Sheets?

<u>Recovered Clue</u>
No, I'm _ _ _ them

Final Answer

257. <u>Mystery</u>
Alcoholic
Beverage

<u>Chapter</u>
Whiskey With a
Beer Chaser

<u>Recovered Clue</u>
Purdue mascot

Final Answer

258. <u>Mystery</u>
Alcoholic
Beverage

<u>Chapter</u>
Hocus Pocus

<u>Recovered Clue</u>
_ra_dab_

Final Answer

259. <u>Mystery</u>
Famous Painting

<u>Chapter</u>
Yodeler's Cousin

<u>Recovered Clue</u>
No, but it's in
the same family

Final Answer

260. <u>Mystery</u>
Indian Nation

<u>Chapter</u>
Squatting Cow

<u>Recovered Clue</u>
Cut the bull
and sit down.

Final Answer

261. <u>Mystery</u>
Popular Phrase

<u>Chapter</u>
Lettuce Entertain
You

<u>Recovered Clue</u>
☺

Final Answer

262. <u>Mystery</u>
Answer to Most
Tabloid Articles

<u>Chapter</u>
_ _ _ *Cares!*

<u>Recovered Clue</u>
What, When, Why,
Where, _ _ _

Final Answer

263. <u>Mystery</u>
English Rock
Group

<u>Chapter</u>
The Men in Blue

<u>Recovered Clue</u>
Bee bite

Final Answer

264. <u>Mystery</u>
American Rock
Band

<u>Chapter</u>
Read Cold *Chili*
Jalepeno's

<u>Recovered Clue</u>
Use your head

Final Answer

265. <u>Mystery</u>
Alternative Rock

<u>Chapter</u>
The Who Could Do
Such a Thing?

<u>Recovered Clue</u>
Halloween

Final Answer

266. Mystery
Hip-Hop/Rap

Chapter
Some are 4 + 37 =

Recovered Clue
Sum r not

Final Answer

267. Mystery
American Rock n'
Roll

Chapter
The Fathers
of Creation

Recovered Clue
The family that
creates together,
invents together.

Final Answer

268. Mystery
Pop Vocal

Chapter
Is Divo Sick?

Recovered Clue
Yes, u could say
that

Final Answer

269. Mystery
New Orleans Jazz

Chapter
Is *Al* Hurt?

Recovered Clue
No, just a little
overweight.

Final Answer

270. Mystery
      British Reggae

      Chapter
      21ˢᵗ & 2ⁿᵈ Letter
      of the Alphabet
      16 x 2.5

      Recovered Clue
      Go with your
      first answer

      Final Answer

271. Mystery
      Post-Grunge

      Chapter
      5 Cents Your
      Change

      Recovered Clue
      Is that all I get,
      a _ _ _?

      Final Answer

272. Mystery
      Actress

      Chapter
      See Illustration

      Recovered Clue
      Jane, get me out
      of this thing!

      Final Answer

273. <u>Mystery</u>
American
Industrial
Music

<u>Chapter</u>
You Need a
Manicurist!

<u>Recovered Clue</u>
¼ yard nails

Final Answer

274. <u>Mystery</u>
Male Composer

<u>Chapter</u>
Ernie
Chiropractor

<u>Recovered Clue</u>
Get out the
bumbershoot!

Final Answer

275. <u>Mystery</u>
Classical
Composer

<u>Chapter</u>
St. Bernard

<u>Recovered Clue</u>
Rollover _ _ _

Final Answer

276. <u>Mystery</u>
Musical Arranger

<u>Chapter</u>
Nelson Twiddle

<u>Recovered Clue</u>
Twiddle minus
the twist

Final Answer

277. <u>Mystery</u>
Biblical Bad Guy

<u>Chapter</u>
Pontius Co-Pilot

<u>Recovered Clue</u>
The head nacho

Final Answer

278. <u>Mystery</u>
Old Testament

<u>Chapter</u>
Book of #'s

<u>Recovered Clue</u>
Put it into words

Final Answer

279. <u>Mystery</u>
Bible

<u>Chapter</u>
They Were so
Gentle

<u>Recovered Clue</u>
The Hebrews?

Final Answer

280. <u>Mystery</u>
Magazine

<u>Chapter</u>
_ _ _ Cookies

<u>Recovered Clue</u>
Look into my
crystal ball.

Final Answer

281. <u>Mystery</u>
Airline

<u>Chapter</u>
First *Atlantic*
Flight

<u>Recovered Clue</u>
The very first

Final Answer

282. <u>Mystery</u>
Cable TV Network

<u>Chapter</u>
Tender Loving
Care

<u>Recovered Clue</u>
Oh come on now!

Final Answer

283. <u>Mystery</u>
Famous Jeweler

<u>Chapter</u>
Carter

<u>Recovered Clue</u>
Louis

Final Answer

284. <u>Mystery</u>
Popular Watch

<u>Chapter</u>
Shortjeans

<u>Recovered Clue</u>
How long does
the battery last?

Final Answer

285. <u>Mystery</u>
World's Finest
Watch

<u>Chapter</u>
Oyster

<u>Recovered Clue</u>
I wear mine to
Wimbledon.

Final Answer

286. <u>Mystery</u>
Canned Meat

<u>Chapter</u>
Unwanted E-Mail

<u>Recovered Clue</u>
Great with
mac & cheese.

Final Answer

287. <u>Mystery</u>
International
Food

<u>Chapter</u>
Maw Maw *Flan*

<u>Recovered Clue</u>
Ma & Pa Kettle

Final Answer

288. <u>Mystery</u>
International
Food

<u>Chapter</u>
Mash-Mish

<u>Recovered Clue</u>
Switch 2 letters

Final Answer

289. Mystery
     International
     Food

     Chapter
     Norway's Version
     of Meatballs

     Recovered Clue
     Is that a flounder
     I see or are you
     just happy 2 c
     me?

     Final Answer

290. Mystery
     International
     Dessert

     Chapter
     Winnie the Pooh
     Cake

     Recovered Clue
     Oh honey,
     honey, honey.

     Final Answer

291. Mystery
     Cfood

     Chapter
     Shrimpy Scamp

     Recovered Clue
     Hay! This shrimp
     is skimpy!

     Final Answer

292. Mystery
     Hand Soap

     Chapter
     _ _ _ and I Like it 2!

     Recovered Clue
     Ireland's favorite
     time of the year

     Final Answer

293. Mystery
Energy Cell

Chapter
I Was Born
Ready!

Recovered Clue
They just keep
multiplying!

Final Answer

294. Mystery
Japanese Cuisine

Chapter
Is Sue a She?

Recovered Clue
Johnny Cash
wants to know

Final Answer

295. Mystery
Meat Dish

Chapter
Strangers in
Paradise

Recovered Clue
Eddie

Final Answer

296. Mystery
International Dish

Chapter
Because, Because
Stew

Recovered Clue
It will help if u r
Hungarian!

Final Answer

297. Mystery
      Indian Food

      Chapter
      Pull My Finger
      Pickle

      Recovered Clue
      That always
      happens when I
      eat _ _ _

      Final Answer

298. Mystery
      Chinese Cuisine

      Chapter
      Cow Slop
      Gal Skillet

      Recovered Clue
      You can't handle
      more than this!

      Final Answer

299. Mystery
      Dessert

      Chapter
      Chocolaty

      Recovered Clue
      Cub Scouts

      Final Answer

300. Mystery
      International
      Food

      Chapter
      Booyawn

      Recovered Clue
      Fort Knox

      Final Answer

301. <u>Mystery</u>
International
Dish

<u>Chapter</u>
Plastered *Pork
and
Cassava Leaves*

<u>Recovered Clue</u>
I'll drink to that!

Final Answer

302. <u>Mystery</u>
Jamaican Dish

<u>Chapter</u>
Idiot Berger

<u>Recovered Clue</u>
Steve Martin as
"The _ _ _."

Final Answer

303. <u>Mystery</u>
Chinese Cuisine

<u>Chapter</u>
Flied Wonton

<u>Recovered Clue</u>
I wish I could
enunciate r's!

Final Answer

304. <u>Mystery</u>
Oral Health

<u>Chapter</u>
Dive! Dive! Take
Us Down to
Peri_ _ _ Depth!

<u>Recovered Clue</u>
Kills bad breath
too!

Final Answer

305. Mystery
Entrepreneur

Chapter
Warren
Smorgasbord

Recovered Clue
Talks too
negative!

Final Answer

306. Mystery
Personal Hygiene

Chapter
Left Tackle

Recovered Clue
Other side of
center

Final Answer

307. Mystery
Vegetable

Chapter
Commission

Recovered Clue
Stringy & boring

Final Answer

308. Mystery
1 of 50 United
States

Chapter
You Make Me Ill &
You Annoy Me!

Recovered Clue
That's all folks!

Final Answer

309. Mystery
Traffic Sign

Chapter
No Liberal *Turn*

Recovered Clue
Often right

Final Answer

310. Mystery
Traffic Sign

Chapter
Sharp
Conservative
Turn

Recovered Clue
Not always right

Final Answer

311. Mystery
Song Title

Chapter
*Papa's Got a
Brand New* _ _ _

Recovered Clue
Paper or plastic?

Final Answer

312. Mystery
Bible

Chapter
Oh My! Sheba
Needs a Bath!

Recovered Clue
That's y her name
is _ _ _

Final Answer

313. Mystery
      Bible

      Chapter
      Read This to Find
      Out How *the*
      Apostles Acted

      Recovered Clue
      Get the Word out!

      Final Answer

314. Mystery
      Popular Flower

      Chapter
      _ _ _ Luego

      Recovered Clue
      Who stole
      my Vega?

      Final Answer

315. Mystery
      Actor

      Chapter
      Guy Hanging on
      the Wall *Carney*

      Recovered Clue
      Norton

      Final Answer

316. Mystery
      Actress

      Chapter
      Tory _ _ _ Bee

      Recovered Clue
      My favorite
      subject in school

      Final Answer

317. Mystery
U.S. Tourist
Attraction

Chapter
Grand Hello o, o,
Down n, n, There
er, er, er

Recovered Clue
Alright! I heard
you
the first time!

Final Answer

318. Mystery
Cable TV

Chapter
Godzilla

Recovered Clue
Talk 2 me b 4 u
get married!

Final Answer

319. Mystery
German Cuisine

Chapter
_ _ _ _ _ _ & Ham

Recovered Clue
Dr. Seuss

Final Answer

320. Mystery
Traffic Sign

Chapter
No Submarine
Races

Recovered Clue
No making out

Final Answer

321. <u>Mystery</u>
Paper Towel

<u>Chapter</u>
Mutiny on the _ _ _

<u>Recovered Clue</u>
It sucks

Final Answer

322. <u>Mystery</u>
Household
Cleaning

<u>Chapter</u>
Y do U Have
2 Lie Saul?

<u>Recovered Clue</u>
You'd better clean
up your act!

Final Answer

323. <u>Mystery</u>
Nursery Rhyme

<u>Chapter</u>
See Illustration

<u>Recovered Clue</u>
That's not the dell
I had in mind.

Final Answer

324. <u>Mystery</u>
Birds of the Air

<u>Chapter</u>
That Bird
Swallowed
the Whole *Tree*

<u>Recovered Clue</u>
I can't believe
I swallowed
the whole thing!

Final Answer

325. <u>Mystery</u>
Alcoholic
Beverage

<u>Chapter</u>
Rita's and
Margaret's
Favorite Drink

<u>Recovered Clue</u>
It should be
named after
them!

Final Answer

326. <u>Mystery</u>
Infectious Disease

<u>Chapter</u>
You Have Ring
Around the Collar

<u>Recovered Clue</u>
a

Final Answer

327. <u>Mystery</u>
America's Pretty
Sleuth

<u>Chapter</u>
Nancy Likes to
Draw

<u>Recovered Clue</u>
She did!

Final Answer

328. Mystery
Foreign Country

Chapter
What Color is
Your Afghan?

Recovered Clue
It only comes
in 1 color silly!

Final Answer

329. Mystery
TV Show

Chapter
Hard-Up
Housewives

Recovered Clue
Get a job!

Final Answer

330. Mystery
Major League
Baseball

Chapter
Excellent Pitcher

Recovered Clue
Ryan Dumpster

Final Answer

331. Mystery
Movie Title

Chapter
The First Polka
in Baghdad

Recovered Clue
T.L.T.I.P.

Final Answer

332. Mystery
Alcoholic
Beverage

Chapter
See Illustration

Recovered Clue
I always keep 1
in my toolbox.

Final Answer

333. Mystery
Birds of the Air

Chapter
Myasian Batman

Recovered Clue
He's not my Asian
_ _ _, he's

_ _ _ _ _ _

Final Answer

334. Mystery
U.S. City

Chapter
Holy _ _ _!

Recovered Clue
Oh! hio

Final Answer

335. <u>Mystery</u>
Cable TV

<u>Chapter</u>
I'm From *New York City* and I'm Glad She's Not My Housewife

<u>Recovered Clue</u>
That's too bad

Final Answer

336. <u>Mystery</u>
Indian Ocean Island

<u>Chapter</u>
I'm Going to be Mad if My Car Runs Out of Gas!

<u>Recovered Clue</u>
They all do over there

Final Answer

337. <u>Mystery</u>
Punk Trio

<u>Chapter</u>
See Illustration

<u>Recovered Clue</u>
I do this when I get my picture taken.

Final Answer

338. <u>Mystery</u>
      Rock n' Roll

      <u>Chapter</u>
      The You're
      What Hurts?

      <u>Recovered Clue</u>
      _ _ _'s on first?

      Final Answer

339. <u>Mystery</u>
      Bible

      <u>Chapter</u>
      Ready, Willing
      and _ _ _

      <u>Recovered Clue</u>
      Able?

      Final Answer

340. <u>Mystery</u>
      Actor

      <u>Chapter</u>
      See Illustration

      <u>Recovered Clue</u>
      Famous brand
      name of

      Final Answer

341. <u>Mystery</u>
Medicine

<u>Chapter</u>
10 Cent Taps

<u>Recovered Clue</u>
I wish it
tasted like beer!

Final Answer

342. <u>Mystery</u>
Russian Leader

<u>Chapter</u>
I Need a Cup of _ _ _
to Get Me Going!

<u>Recovered Clue</u>
Come on Joe,
quit stalling!

Final Answer

343. <u>Mystery</u>
Actress

<u>Chapter</u>
See Illustration

<u>Recovered Clue</u>
Gloria "Hungry
Man"

Final Answer

344. <u>Mystery</u>
Country Western
Song Title

<u>Chapter</u>
You *Fight*
Like a Girl!

<u>Recovered Clue</u>
A little less
of you please!

Final Answer

345. <u>Mystery</u>
Oral Hygiene

<u>Chapter</u>
Juicy Fruit
is My Fave!

<u>Recovered Clue</u>
Da z!

Final Answer

346. <u>Mystery</u>
Actress

<u>Chapter</u>
See Illustration

<u>Recovered Clue</u>
Is this Victoria's
office?

Final Answer

347. Mystery
     TV Show

     Chapter
     Whose Body
     Part is This?

     Recovered Clue
     It's Dr. Gray's

     Final Answer

348. Mystery
     Actress

     Chapter
     Truck Rental

     Recovered Clue
     Y don't u ask
     Nona?

     Final Answer

349. Mystery
     Movie Title

     Chapter
     See Illustration

     Recovered Clue
     Now I can go
     to the vet!

     Final Answer

350. <u>Mystery</u>
European Tourist
Attraction

<u>Chapter</u>
Go to Paris to Get

<u>Recovered Clue</u>
An eye full of
that tower

Final Answer

351. <u>Mystery</u>
Mythology

<u>Chapter</u>
That Jar
Belongs To

<u>Recovered Clue</u>
Make sure you
don't open it!

Final Answer

352. <u>Mystery</u>
South Korean
City

<u>Chapter</u>
Filet of _ _ _

<u>Recovered Clue</u>
Huey Lewis has
"Heart & Soul."

Final Answer

THE FINAL ANSWERS

1. Eminem

2. The Bold and the Beautiful

3. Ty Cobb

4. Tootsie

5. Grasshopper

6. Mary Had a Little Lamb

7. Fidel Castro

8. Shania Twain

9. Sheryl Crow

10. Iraq

11. 60 Minutes

12. Home Improvement

13. Babe Ruth

14. Arnold Palmer

15. Rain Man

16. Psycho

17. Lucille

18. Yasir Arafat

19. Gucci

20. Natalie Wood

21. Marvin Gaye

22. Leave it to Beaver

23. Who Framed Roger Rabbit?

24. Polident

25. Minute Maid

26. Uncle Ben's

27. Zits

28. Pasta

29. Bed Bath & Beyond

30. Job

31. Jeremiah

32. Dizzy Gillespie

33. Knockout Punch

34. Like a Virgin

35. If You Could Read My Mind

36. Rin Tin Tin

37. Rodeo Drive

38. Joe Montana

39. Longfellow

40. Ajax

41. Eric Bana

42. Clint Eastwood

43. Dr. Phil

44. Judy Garland

45. Drew Barrymore

46. Discover

47. Wonton Soup

48. The Onion

49. The Swine Flu

50. Thyme

51. Ketchup

52. Skewer

53. Tamale

54. Smothered Chicken

55. UCLA

56. Picadilly Square

57. Adolf Hitler	58. Louis Pasteur
59. Dusty Baker	60. Vincent Van Gogh
61. Cellphone	62. Gwen Stefani
63. Newfoundland	64. Timbuktu
65. Scrubs	66. 2 ½ Men
67. Braden Looper	68. The Farmstead
69. Midnight Cowboy	70. Lucy
71. Wheel of Fortune	72. Influenza
73. Nicotine	74. Bladder
75. Frostbite	76. Cat Scratch Fever
77. Shingles	78. Joan Jett
79. Billy Crystal	80. Christopher Plummer
81. Reuben	82. Usher
83. Peptic Ulcer	84. Ziggy
85. U2	86. Uruguay
87. Bora Bora	88. New York City

89. Wales

90. Mr. Rogers Neighborhood

91. The Electric Company

92. Mark Cuban

93. Facebook

94. Verne Gagne

95. The Chicago White Sox

96. O.J. Simpson

97. Nick Faldo

98. Guy Lafleur

99. Bruce Jenner

100. Earl Monroe

101. Edwin Moses

102. Ivana Trump

103. Dick Butkus

104. The Pelican Brief

105. Valley Girl

106. Legally Blonde

107. MTV

108. Malcolm in the Middle

109. I Want My MTV

110. Walk Like an Egyptian

111. Bearded Collie

112. Don Ho

113. Cross Traffic Does Not Stop

114. Speed Limit 65

115. Tiger Woods

116. Tuba

117. Bassoon

118. Rooster

119. Chow Chow

120. I Only Have Eyes for You

121. Martini

122. Sex on the Beach

123. Betsy Ross

124. Rembrandt

125. Ric Flair

126. Dick the Bruiser

127. Lex Luger

128. Obesity

129. Kleenex

130. Evaporated Milk

131. Cantaloupe

132. The O'Reilly Factor

133. Mario Lemieux

134. The Cougar

135. All My Children

136. ESPN

137. Caffeine

138. One Life to Live

139. David Spade

140. Marcus Aurelius

141. Brutus

142. Apollo

143. Hearing Aid

144. Dopamine

145. Gingivitis

146. Acne

147. Pneumonia

148. Triceps

149. Exit Only

150. Cosmos

151. 50 Cent

152. Carrie Underwood

153. Urinary Tract

154. Def Jam

155. Long-Eared Owl

156. Rifleman

157. Bluejay

158. Painted Bunting

159. Rook

160. Caucasian

161. Hernia

162. Alcoholism

163. Antibiotics

164. Rocky Mountain Spotted Fever

165. Rectum

166. Flat Feet

167. Tennis Elbow

168. Kate Moss

169. Sandra O

170. Buck Owens

171. Marilyn Manson

172. Tammy Wynette

173. Amy Winehouse

174. Denver

175. Brussels

176. Bombay

177. Cuba

178. Canary Islands

179. Boston

180. Hawaii

181. Cologne

182. Greece

183. Santa Monica

184. London

185. Louisville

186. Iran

187. New Dehli

188. Wichita

189. Minneapolis

190. Crash Investigation Site

191. Cary Grant

192. Kevin Bacon

193. John Candy

194. Penn State

195. Impatiens

196. Psychology Today

197. Pintail Duck

198. Hairy Woodpecker

199. Mistletoebird

200. No Public Dumping

201. General Hospital

202. Bald Eagle

203. George Burns

204. Paul Newman

205. Omar Shariff

206. George Clooney

207. David Letterman

208. How I Met Your Mother

209. Denny Crane

210. Bette Midler

211. The E! True
     Hollywood Story

212. Abbie Cornish

213. Kate Gosselin

214. Farrah Fawcett

215. Shirley Temple

216. Leighton Meester

217. Hall & Oates

218. Chuck Berry

219. Stevie Wonder

220. Mick Jagger

221. Ludacris

222. Soulja Boy

223. DMX

224. Zac Efron

225. Garth Brooks

226. Cat Stevens

227. Frank Zappa

228. Flo-rida

229. Miley Cyrus

230. LL Cool J

231. Roger Miller

232. The Family Feud

233. Lady Gaga

234. Mary Mary

235. Deelishus

236. Helen Reddy

237. Indianapolis

238. Turkey

239. The Mentalist

240. Chattanooga

241. Tijuana

242. Phoenix

243. Tucson

244. Helsinki

245. Manila

246. Aspen

247. Rugrats

248. TNT

249. The 700 Club

250. Alewife

251. Bad to the Bone

252. Stoopid

253. Poker Face

254. Black Russian

255. Coconut Milk

256. Between the Sheets

257. Boilermaker

258. Abracadabra

259. Whistler's Mother

260. Sitting Bull

261. Let Us Entertain You

262. Who cares?

263. The Police

264. Red Hot Chili Peppers

265. The Smashing Pumpkins

266. Sum 41

267. The Mothers of Invention

268. ILDIVO

269. Al Hirt

270. UB40

271. Nickelback

272. Jane Russell

273. Nine Inch Nails

274. Burt Bacharach

275. Beethoven

276. Nelson Riddle

277. Pontius Pilate

278. Book of Numbers

279. Gentiles

280. Fortune

281. Virgin Atlantic

282. TLC

283. Cartier

284. Longines

285. Rolex

286. SPAM

287. Paw Paw Flan

288. Mish-Mash

289. Fishballs

290. Honey Cake

291. Shrimp Scampi

292. Irish Spring

293. Eveready Energizer

294. Sushi

295. Meatloaf

296. Cous Cous Stew

297. Cabbage Pickle

298. Moo Goo Gai Pan

299. Brownies

300. Bouillon

301. Stewed Pork and Cassava Leaves

302. Jerk Burger

303. Fried Wonton

304. Scope

305. Warren Buffett

306. Right Guard

307. Celery

308. Illinois

309. No Left Turn

310. Sharp Right Turn

311. Papa's Got a Brand New Bag

312. Bathsheba

313. Acts of the Apostles

314. Hosta

315. Art Carney

316. Tory Spelling

317. Grand Canyon

318. Bridezilla

319. Green Eggs

320. No Parking

321. Bounty

322. Lysol

323. Farmer in the Dell

324. Tree Swallow

325. Margarita

326. Cholera

327. Nancy Drew

328. Afghanistan

329. Desperate Housewives

330. Ryan Dempster

331. The Last Tango in Paris

332. Screwdriver

333. Eurasian Robin

334. Toledo

335. The Real Housewives of New York City

336. Madagascar

337. Blink 182

338. The Who

339. Abel

340. Burt Reynolds

341. Dimetapp

342. Joe Stalin

343. Gloria Swanson

344. Fight Like a Girl

345. Gum Disease

346. Victoria Principal

347. Grey's Anatomy

348. Winona Ryder

349. Slum Dog Millionaire

350. Eiffel Tower

351. Pandora

352. Seoul

LaVergne, TN USA
17 March 2010
176297LV00002B/1/P